natural English

intermediate listening booklet
Ruth Gairns & Stuart Redman
with Louise Williams

in this listening booklet
- tapescripts for all student's book listening sections
- optional listening and pronunciation activities, plus tapescript based exercises. Use these in addition to the student's book listening activities.

use the listening booklet when you want to
- do a bit of extra listening
- use the tapescript
- do some pronunciation practice

student's CD also available
ISBN 0194383857

OXFORD
UNIVERSITY PRESS

0.1

Conversation 1

S We've met before, haven't we?

B Yes, I ... I'm really sorry, I don't remember your name.

S Sophie.

B Sophie. That's right, yeah.

S And you're Brian, aren't you?

B Yep, yep, yep, yeah.

S Yeah, yeah. We did the er, we did that other course last year ...

B That's right, yeah. (Yeah) It was about this time of year too, (yeah) actually, wasn't it, yeah.

S And I seem to remember you'd just had a kid, hadn't you?

B Yes, that's right, yeah, yeah, little girl.

S Little girl. How is she?

B She's very well. (Hmm) Yes, yes, growing really quickly ...

Conversation 2

M I mean, I think the ancient history of the Greeks is fascinating (Hmm) so to, to study it (Hi) on a course like this ...

D Hi! Tyler.

T Deborah! Hello!

D Hello!

T How are you?

D I'm very well, thank you. How are you?

T Fine, thanks. Did you, did you drive here tonight?

D I did, yes.

T Do you, do you know Mike?

M Hello.

D Yes, we already know each other.

M Yes, we did a course together last year.

T Oh!

D That's right.

M So, here we are for the Greeks then!

D Nice to see you!

M And you.

1.1

Right, right, today we're going to look at the economic situation in Europe.

beep beep

Look, I said no mobile phones in class!

But Miss, it's my granny – she's just fallen downstairs.

beep beep

I SAID NO MOBILES!

It's the hospital – they want me to go and give blood – it's urgent.

beep beep

I SAID NO ...

But Miss, it's my father – I've never met him, and he wants to see me.

beep beep

Listen, Crystal, how many times do I have to tell you? You peel the potatoes and boil them for 15 minutes. It's not that complicated! OK, but don't bother me again.

Now then ...

beep beep

Miss! Don't forget the salt ...

1.2

... yes, we often talk about fashion. How about you, Pedro?

... I never talk about current affairs. What about you, Yoko?

1.3

Marcella

M I was queueing up for some tickets the other day, and er, there was a fellow beside me who was a motorbike courier ...

R Oh, right!

M ... and I needed to have a look at his A to Z, because I needed to find my way somewhere, and er, it turned out that he was actually a doctor from Colombia ...

R Oh, right!

M ... and he had just decided to change his life for a while and come over and try something completely different, and er, he was just talking about how different it was, you know, his life in Colombia and being a ... a motorbike courier here, he was fascinating, actually, and it was so funny ...

Nigel

N I was having this terrible conversation at work yesterday ...

L Yeah?

N ... with this man called Malcolm from the accounts department ...

L Oh yeah?

N ... and we were talking about Angela, who's my supervisor, and I was saying that she's being really horrible to people recently ...

L Is she?

N ... the young people in the office, she's, she's just being really nasty to them, and I was going on and on and he was just not saying anything, and just smiling, you know. Anyway it only turns out he's just got engaged to her!

L Oh no!

N I couldn't believe it!

L Oh, no!

N I'm going to be looking for a new job, aren't I!

L Oh, maybe not. You never know ...

1.2

a Listen to the cassette. Notice the intonation.

b Practise saying the phrases, paying attention to the intonation.

c Now change the topics and the names, for example

... yes, we often talk about cooking.

How about you, Tim?

1.3

a Listen to the conversations. Circle phrases where Ralph and Lily show that they are listening. Underline phrases where Lily shows surprise or horror.

b Look at the tapescript. Find another way to express the phrases in bold.

1 I was **standing in a queue** for some tickets **a few days ago**
2 there was a fellow **next to** me
3 I needed to **check in** his A to Z
4 he'd just decided to change his life **for a period of time**
5 she's **behaving very unpleasantly towards** people

Check with the answer key.

one

1.4
Juliet
J I was in a pub the other night, ...
R Hmm.
J ... and I had this really extraordinary conversation with this man. He, he was quite a young guy, he had a ... a shaved head ...
R Right.
J ... and he just came out and told me that he was a bank robber.
R What?!
J Yeah, exactly, and, and, he'd already been in prison for ten years before, but while he was in prison, he'd he'd had this idea of, that the thing to do was be, would be to rob banks ...
R Right.
J ... because before he'd been like, a house burglar, now he was going to start robbing banks, and it was just, I couldn't believe that he would come out and tell this to a complete stranger in a pub. Mad!
R I know. What was he thinking?

1.5
Excuse me, is anyone sitting here?
Sorry, have you got the time, please?
I think we've met before, haven't we?
It's really hot, isn't it?
Are you going all the way to San Francisco?

1.6
I'm going to spend a week in the desert.
A Oh, really? How interesting!
B Ooh, how exciting!
C That sounds great.

1.7
C Good party, isn't it?
E Great, yeah, I'm having a really good time. Are you?
C Yeah, yeah, I'm enjoying it, yeah.
E So erm ...
C So what do you, what do you do?
E Oh, well, erm, I'm ... I'm still at school, actually, and I'm er, I'm studying physics, chemistry and biology.
C Oh, right, OK, so what are you hoping to do, then, when you leave school?
E Well, I'd like to go to university, erm, to, er, study medicine ...
C Oh, right.
E ... and er, I'm thinking of doing part of the course maybe in the, in the States.
C Oh, right, that sounds interesting. (Yeah) Is that because there's better teaching there, better courses or universities there?
E Well, no, I just like the idea of, of going overseas and training a bit abroad.
C Hm, getting a bit of experience over there. (Yeah) Yeah, that's very valuable. I did a year out too.

E Did you?
C Yeah, yeah, studied in Australia, actually.
E Did you?
C Yeah, that was good.
E I think, you know, I just, just like the idea of, of being with people from a different country, (Right) and, you know, spending some time in another city.
C Yeah, no, I think ...

1.8
A I'm going to stay with my uncle.
B I'm planning to rent a car.
C I'm hoping to get a part-time job.
D I'm thinking of going abroad this winter.

1.9
L Hello.
A Hi.
L I'm Lola.
A Ah, Andrew.
L Where are you from?
A Er, Glasgow.
L Oh, in Scotland.
A Yes, yes.
L Oh, that's lovely.
A Well, it's, it's quite nice.
L I, I, I'm from Austria.
A Oh, really? Ah, how interesting. Whereabouts?
L From Vienna.
A Ah, it's beautiful, I believe.
L It is.
A I've never been there. Are you travelling by yourself?
L Oh, yes.
A Me, too.
L Are you meeting somebody, perhaps?
A No, I'm just going on holiday by myself.
L Oh!
A And you, you're meeting somebody, maybe?
L Well, I hope so!
A I think probably we all hope that!
L Well, it's er, it's quite embarrassing actually, I'm, er, I'm on a blind date. I'm going to meet a boy!
A Oh, how fascinating!
L Well, I'm er, I'm hoping he's going to be there. (Well!) I have this, this terrible picture that maybe when I get there, well, he won't be there.
A Oh, I'm sure he will. It's ... it's very adventurous you know, travelling all this way on a blind date.
L Well, I think we do have something in common. (Hm?) We're both acrobats ...
A Really?
L ... yes ... what do you do?
A Oh, ... I'm very boring, I'm a dentist.
L Oh! I'm really scared of dentists.
A Och, there's not a lot to be scared about.

1.4

a Look at the tapescript. Read and listen as far as the words *bank robber*.

Notice how Juliet stresses the most important words.

b Listen again to the first part of her story and underline the stressed words, for example

I was in a <u>pub</u> the other <u>night</u> ...

Check with the answer key.

c Now try to read the tapescript, paying attention to the stressed words. First read at your own speed without listening to the cassette. Then try to read while you play the cassette.

1.4

Look at these words from tapescript 1.4. Notice how we pronounce the letters in bold.

/æ/	/eɪ/	/ɑː/	/ə/
m**a**n	sh**a**ved	st**a**rt	cig**a**rette

Put the words in the box into four groups, according to the pronunciation of the letters in bold.

m**a**d	f**a**ther	**a**sleep
t**a**ke	p**a**rk	ex**a**ctly
c**a**me	b**a**nk	burgl**a**r
m**a**rket	**a**go	str**a**nger
convers**a**tion	p**a**th	st**a**nd
import**a**nt		

1.5

a Listen to the cassette. Notice the intonation of the questions.

Excuse me, is anyone sitting here?

Sorry, have you got the time, please?

I think we've met before, haven't we?

It's really hot, isn't it?

Are you going all the way to San Francisco?

b Practise saying the questions, paying attention to the intonation.

1.6

a When we want to show we are interested, we often make some of our words longer, by exaggerating certain sounds. Listen and notice how some of the vowel sounds are exaggerated.

/ ɪə /	/ uː /	/ eɪ /
really	Ooh	great

b Practise saying the phrases. Exaggerate the words *really*, *Ooh*, and *great*, so that you sound really interested!

1.7

a Look at the start of the conversation between Clive and Emma. Notice how the words they use are very similar in meaning. This type of repetition helps to keep the conversation going.

Clive   **Good** party, isn't it?
Emma   **Great**, yeah, **I'm having a really good time.** Are you?
Clive   Yeah, yeah, **I'm enjoying it,** yeah.

b Their conversation has two main topics

studying
going abroad

Circle the words connected with studying in one colour, and the words connected with going abroad in a different colour. Notice how the coloured circles help to hold the conversation together.
The next time you listen to a conversation in English, listen for repetition of words and ideas.

1.8

a Listen to the examples. Notice the stressed words.

I'm <u>going</u> to <u>stay</u> with my <u>uncle</u>.
I'm <u>planning</u> to <u>rent</u> a <u>car</u>.
I'm <u>hoping</u> to get a <u>part-time job</u>.
I'm <u>thinking</u> of <u>going</u> <u>abroad</u> this <u>winter</u>.

b Listen and repeat, paying attention to the stressed words.

1.9

a To keep their conversation going Lola and Andrew ask and answer questions, for example

Lola   How are you?
Andrew   I'm, I'm very well, thank you.

They also use positive adjectives to show they are interested in what the other person is saying, for example

Lola   Oh that's <u>lovely</u>.

b Look at the tapescript of Lola and Andrew's conversation and find examples of

the questions they ask
the positive adjectives they use

2.1

There's this man, OK, and he's travelling across the desert, and he suddenly finds he hasn't got any water left. So he's starting to get worried, and he's very thirsty, but luckily, a man comes towards him on a camel.

So he says to the man, 'I'm thirsty. Have you got any water?' and the other man says, 'No, I haven't, but I've got a wonderful selection of ties. Would you like to buy one?' So the other man says, 'No, of course not!' and the man rides away on his camel.

After about another hour or two, he's desperately thirsty and he sees a beautiful 5-star hotel. So he slowly goes up the steps, crying 'Water! Water!' and the hotel manager says, 'I'm sorry, sir, you can't come in here without a tie.'

2.2
Julia

Well, erm, last year, when I was in India, erm, myself and my boyfriend wanted to go from one side of the river to the other side of the river (Mm) and so we asked this man to take us in his coracle – which is, I don't know if you know what they are (No!) but they're a <u>tiny</u> boat, they're <u>circular</u>, almost like erm, a dish really (Oh) and erm, so we stepped in very carefully, there were three of us in this boat and erm, off we went, and it was just beautiful, it was so <u>peaceful</u> and <u>quiet</u> and all we could hear was the water, and it was a really beautiful experience (Yeah) until suddenly the water started whirling round and round and round, and so our little boat started going round and round, and we were really <u>frightened</u> because water started coming in (Oh no!) to the coracle and it was going faster and faster, and the man seemed out of control and we could hear the water and it was splashing us (Ah!) and we seemed to be sinking (Oh) and eventually he pulled us to the side and er, we managed to get out, so it was, it was exciting and it was different, but erm, it was a bit too <u>frightening</u>.

Marcella

A couple of years ago, I took this trip to Africa, (Hmm) and I flew directly to Victoria Falls (Oh, extraordinary) oh, absolutely extraordinary, and I decided to take, there's a special trip you can take on a microlite (Yeah) which is, it's like a hang glider (Yeah, I know) but it has a tiny little engine. (Hmm) I can't believe how wonderful it was. You sit behind a pilot, and you go up for about half an hour, and you, you sort of zigzag across the falls and there's masses of this steam, it's just so beautiful and the pilot points out to you the various animals down below – there can be hippo or zebra, elephant – oh! it's just so beautiful, it it's, like a piece of magic – you know what I mean? (Yeah) And you can't hear anything up there, it's completely silent, you ... you don't notice the little sound of the engine, because it's very tiny anyway, and er, it's the nearest thing to flying, you know, it's really, really fantastic.

2.3
Juliet

J   The summer before last, I, I took a holiday in er, Cuba and I spent some time in the capital city, Havana, (Right) and one of the cheapest and best ways to get around the city is in these cycle rickshaws and erm, what you have is, you have, you have like a little cabin (Uhuh) attached to the bicycle and you, and you can seat two people in this, in this little ...

E   Is it comfortable?

J   Some of them are – it depends. Sometimes the seat is quite well ... erm, you know, is quite soft, (Yeah) sometimes it can be quite hard and it makes for a very bumpy ride (Ah, right) erm, and also the streets are full of holes, (Hmm) and it ... and it can make for again for a very bumpy ride.

E   And it must be very hot too.

J   Yeah, it gets very hot in er, very hot and very humid, er but you know sometimes they can get quite a good speed up, and then the breeze, you know, cools you down a little bit, but it's a great way to see the city.

E   Would you go again?

J   Definitely, it's a wonderful place, great music.

2.4

A   I think the most important thing is good accommodation.

B   Hot, sunny weather's a priority for me.

C   I think you have to have some adventure and excitement.

D   You don't need great beaches.

2.5

1   I'm having problems with the bathroom taps – they keep dripping and I can't turn them off.

2   The TV isn't working properly – and we can only get one channel.

3   The phone's out of order – and I need to ring my family.

4   The washing machine's leaking – and there's water all over the floor.

5   The fan isn't working – and the living room is incredibly hot.

6   I'm having problems locking the front door – I can't turn the key.

7   There's something wrong with the iron – it's just not getting hot enough.

2.2

a Look at the words underlined in Julia's story. Listen again. How are they pronounced? Practise saying them.

b You can describe things using *it's like ...* (= *it's similar to ...*), for example

a stretch limousine *is like* a very long car

Look at the tapescript. How do they describe the coracle and the microlite?

2.3

When Juliet tells Eric about her holiday in Cuba, she stresses the most important words.

Listen to the introduction to her story (until Eric says *Is it comfortable?*) with the tapescript. Underline as many stressed words as you can. Listen again, if you want.
Check your words with the answer key.

The next time you listen to spoken English, try to focus on the stressed words – it will help you to understand the general meaning.

2.3

Look at these words. Notice how we pronounce the letters in bold.

/iː/ /e/ /ə/ /eɪ/
sp**ee**d b**e**st wond**er**ful gr**ea**t

Put the words in the box into four groups, according to the pronunciation of the letters in bold.

r**e**d	cin**e**ma	th**e**se
gr**ey**	s**ea**t	ch**ea**p
th**e**m	aft**er**	st**ea**k
br**ea**k	w**eigh**	int**er**national
d**e**finite	p**eo**ple	g**e**t
moth**er**		

2.4

Look at these words from the sentences.

important
accommodation
priority
adventure
excitement

a In each word, underline the stressed syllable.

b Listen and check. Then check with the answer key.

2.6

Conversation 1

CM Come in! Oh, hello.

G Hello.

CM What can I do for you?

G Um, my washing machine isn't working properly.

CM Oh, dear. Erm, since when?

G Since yesterday.

CM Right.

G We tried it yesterday for the first time and it isn't working. After ten minutes, it just stops.

CM Uhum, so the light does come on?

G The light comes on ...

CM Fine ...

G ... yes, and then it just stops, and also I realize that the powder isn't being used.

CM Right, well, listen, I'm not an expert on this. I think what we'll have to do is ... oh, can I just ask you, how long are you here for? Are you here for another week, or is it two weeks ... just another week?

G Yes, it's one more week.

CM I tell you what I'll do, I'll get someone in, first thing in the morning ...

G Yes ...

CM ... and ask them to have a look at it. How's that?

G That's great.

CM OK.

G Yes, what time will that be?

CM About 9.30.

G OK, lovely, thank you very much.

CM No problem.

G Thank you.

Conversation 2

G Hi, I'm sorry to bother you, but there's something wrong with the front door lock.

CM Oh, yes, what is it?

G Well, it seems to be broken. I had trouble getting in last night when I came home with some food that I wanted to cook for dinner, and it took forever to get in.

CM And is the problem with the ... the door itself or ... ?

G No, it's the lock itself. I don't know exactly what it is (Yes) but it just doesn't seem to work right, and erm ...

CM Does the key fit into the lock, erm ... ?

G Yes, it does, but I ... I just had so much trouble getting in last night, (Yes) you know, last week it was the kitchen tap, and now it's the front door, (But) it's a little difficult, really.

CM But the kitchen tap is, that problem is finished.

G That's been fixed.

CM Sorted out.

G Yes. But maybe, could you get someone to have a look at it?

CM Oh, yes indeed. Er ... are you in later on today?

G Yes, later on will be fine.

CM No problem – I'll send somebody round.

G OK, thanks.

2.6

If you can identify the stages in a conversation, you will be able to understand it better.

a Look at conversation 1. In this conversation, there are five different stages

1 opening the conversation
2 stating the problem
3 giving details of the problem
4 solving the problem
5 closing the conversation

b Read the conversation. Try to identify the different stages. Check with the answer key.

3.1

Oh, it's such a perfect day, I'm glad I spent it with you ...

Be quiet, will you! I'm reading.

Oh, such a perfect day ...

BYRON, SHUT UP!

You just keep me hanging on ...

YOU'RE SINGING OUT OF TUNE! IT'S AWFUL SITTING NEXT TO YOU.

Well, I'm next to you, and you stink.

I'll get you later!

Oh, hi. Yeah, homework for the music class? What? The lyrics to *Perfect Day*? Aaargh! I'd completely forgotten.

For tomorrow ... do you know the words? Have you got the CD?

No, me neither.

OK! Sing!

3.2

1 A I like this one.
   B Yeah, me too.
2 A I don't like this.
   B No, me neither.
3 A I like this one.
   B Really? I don't.
4 A I don't like this.
   B Really? I do.

3.3 (3 minutes)

Perfect Day   lemonade

Just a perfect day, drink orangeade in the park
And then later when it gets dark, we go home
Just a perfect day, see animals in the zoo
Then later the moon is new, and then home
                a movie too

Chorus

Oh! it's such a perfect day
            glad
I'm mad I spent it with you
Oh! such a perfect day
         just
You must keep me hanging on   (ois)

Just a perfect day, problems are left at home
Weekenders on our own, it's just fun
                        such
Just a perfect day, you made me forget my
wealth self
I thought I was someone else, someone good

Chorus

You're going to reap just what you sow
You're going to reap just what you sow
You're going to reap just what you sow
You're going to reap just what you sow

3.4

Lorelei

C So, how long have you been an actor?
L Oh, long time, long time now, about 20 years.
C Twenty years! (Mm) Gosh! (Can you

imagine) So you must have done a lot of work!
L I have, I've done all kinds of work as well, I've done, er radio, quite a lot of radio, I've done a fair bit of television, I've done a lot of er, voice-over work (aha) – I've been the voice of a slot machine in Las Vegas; I think that's probably the funniest job I ever had. And I've done the voices for a lot of cartoon series ...
C Oh, right ...
L ... which I enjoy.
C Oh, good. Any, any films?
L Yeah, I've done a few of those recently, I did a film called *Notting Hill* ...
C Oh, right, yeah.
L ... which was great, it had Julia Roberts and Hugh Grant in it, and they were tremendous fun to work with, and I really, really enjoyed it.
C Oh, right. And were they nice? I mean, were they nice to you?
L They were very nice I'm happy to say, because you hear horror stories, don't you, about big Hollywood stars, but they were, no, they were both fantastic.

Chris

T Chris, how long have you been an actor?
C Ooh! About ... just over 12 years, I think.
T Right.
C 12 years, I've done loads of work in that time.
T Yeah, and what sort of things, for example?
C Well ... erm I ... I ... I've done short films, I've made short films, I've er, written a lot of things, for comedy for television, and stuff like that ...
T Yes, theatre – have you done theatre?
C Oh, yes, I've written plays as well as, as well as, er, performed in them.
T Yes.
C And er, and I've done a ... an awful lot of commercials. (Yes) I've done a lot of commercials for here, er for everywhere, in fact, all sorts of countries all over the world. Erm, one of my favourites, er, was for a well-known English beer.
T Yes, tell us!
C Er, well, the good thing about it was it was recorded in Los Angeles! Fantastic, it was, and er ...
T When was that?
C Oh, that's a few years ago now, but er, the good thing was, I had to go in a sports car, under a series of lorries.
T Oh that sounds fun!
C It was great fun, and I was just in the passenger seat, and they had a stunt driver, who'd worked with Arnold Schwarzenegger, (Aha) Sylvester Stallone, and he drove this sports car all the way under these six lorries, and it was a ... a fantastic experience.
T Sounds very exciting!

3.4

a Look at the two conversations.
   Underline three phrases containing
   the word *fun*. What does *fun* mean?
   Now look at the natural English
   box on page 38 of the student's
   book.

b Cover the tapescript. Which words
   could go in the gaps?

Lorelei
1 I've done all _____ of work as
   well …
2 I've done _____ a lot of
   radio …
3 I've done a fair _____ of
   television …
4 Any films?
   Yes, I've done a _____ of
   those …

Chris
5 I've done _____ of work in
   that time …
6 I've written a _____ of
   things …
7 I've done an _____ lot of
   commercials …
8 … in fact, all _____ of
   countries all over the world …

Check with the tapescript.

3.5

Ju ... the great thing about acting really for me is the variety, erm ...

Jo What do you mean by that?

Ju Well, er, I've done lots of different things, I've done erm, radio, erm I've done television jobs, I've been in quite a few television programmes, (Oh, really?) erm I've done theatre, erm, I've even done some work in advertising. I did a commercial in Italy erm, a while ago.

Jo Was that fun?

Ju It was, it was great fun. Erm, I've met some interesting people. Erm, so yes, I've had a, I've had a really good time.

Jo Go on, tell us – who've you met?

Ju Who've I met? Erm, well, I did a ... a play with Alan Rickman a few years ago, I did *Hamlet* with him, (Oh, right) and I've done, erm, I did a film with Bob Hoskins a couple of years ago. Erm, I've had a good time – it's a great job. Yeah.

3.6

I can remember learning to swim very clearly.
I can just remember learning to ride a bike.
I can't remember learning to tie my shoelaces at all.

3.7

1 When I was at primary school, we used to write stories, and then draw pictures to go with them.

2 When I was a child, I used to enjoy our painting lessons at school, but I never liked going round art galleries.

3 When I left school, I started a History of Art course at university, but I didn't finish it.

4 I remember when I was younger, I drew pictures of my family all the time. Oh, my mum really loved that.

5 When I was in my early twenties, I worked in a museum for six months. Must have been the best time of my life.

3.5

a Listen to the interview with Julia. How many times does she use the present perfect to describe an experience she has had? Use the tapescript to help you, if you want.

b Listen again and notice how she stresses the past participle and the object of the sentence.

I've <u>done</u> <u>radio</u>
I've <u>done</u> <u>television</u> <u>jobs</u>
I've <u>done</u> <u>theatre</u>
I've <u>met</u> some <u>interesting</u> <u>people</u>

c Now practise saying these phrases. Think about where you put the stress.

3.5

Look at these words. Notice how we pronounce the letters in bold.

/ɪ/	/aɪ/	/iː/
film	time	magazine

Put the words in the box into three groups, according to the pronunciation of the letters in bold.

qu**i**te	pol**i**ce	**I**taly
p**i**zza	**i**nteresting	sard**i**ne
wh**i**le	d**i**d	sk**ii**ng
th**i**ng	h**i**de	h**igh**
d**i**fferent	n**igh**t	advert**i**se

3.6

a Look at the examples. Notice how we often use the schwa /ə/ to pronounce unstressed vowel sounds (indicated in bold below).

I c**a**n rememb**er** learning t**o** swim very clearly.

I c**a**n just rememb**er** learning t**o** ride a bike.

I can't rememb**er** learning t**o** tie my shoelaces **a**t all.

b Practise saying the phrases. Use the schwa /ə/ for unstressed syllables.

3.7

a When we talk about the past, we often use a time clause, for example

When I was at primary school …

Underline the time clauses in the tapescript. Check with the answer key.

b Time clauses are not usually the most important part of the sentence, so we say them quite quickly. Practise saying the time clauses. How quickly can you say them?

4.1

So there's a man going to work and he's walking through the park, and he sees a kangaroo hopping about the park. So he thinks, 'Well, I can't just leave it there,' so he goes to the police station, and he says to them, 'What shall I do? There's a kangaroo hopping about the park.' And the policeman says, 'Er, well, sir, I think you should take it to the zoo.'

So erm, a few days later the policeman is walking down the street, and he suddenly sees the man with the kangaroo, standing at a bus stop together.

So the policeman goes over to them, and he says, 'Erm, excuse me, sir, I thought I told you to take that kangaroo to the zoo!'

And the man grins at him and says, ' Er, yes, we went to the zoo yesterday. I suggested the zoo again today, but he said he'd prefer to go to the cinema.'

4.2

1 A Would he like to go to the zoo?
   B No, he'd prefer to go to the cinema.
2 A Shall I get her a present?
   B I think she'd rather have money.

4.3

1 A My name's McMurdoch.
   B Pardon?
2 A So here's my number – it's 8764 3379.
   B Sorry, I didn't quite catch that.
3 A Do you want ice in it?
   B Sorry?
4 A OK, that's Oundle, O–U–N–D–L–E.
   B Sorry, I missed that.

4.4

I'm really interested in sports programmes.
I'm not very interested in drama series.
I'm definitely not interested in quiz shows.

4.5

Ma Mike, what particular ideas have you had about this?

Mi Well, there are two that I particularly like. (Yep) I like erm, 'New Wheels', which is the programme, er, about the choice of a next, a new car, (Oh, indeed, yeah) which affects everybody. I know it's a thing that mostly men are interested in, but I think with a woman presenter, we can actually get women involved in that, and I also like erm, er, the programme, er, 'Survival' about surviving in the rainforest (Yes, hmm) ... which I think would appeal to all age groups, and in fact would also, I think will be er, quite cheap to make, because it's just one person with a camera.

Ma That's a good point, yes. Eric, what do you think?

E Well, erm, I like this fashion model idea. I think it would appeal to both, er, men and women. Young women would want to know, perhaps, er, they see so many images in the magazines, and they may indeed be interested in, in getting in the business themselves, and men naturally like to look at pretty women on television – this is natural, we all know about that. (Hmm) I like the, er, rainforest survival programme too, I think that could make a very interesting programme. (Hmm) Beautiful shots of wildlife, plus the idea of ...

Mi It's always popular.

E ... yes, of the struggle of one person's survival.

Ma Hmm. I was more attracted to the programme about hypnosis ...

Mi Really?

Ma ... because these days, people are trying to give up smoking, or lose weight, and they've tried so many options (Yes) and apparently hypnosis can work if you, if you apply yourself to it, I quite like that idea (Hmm). Erm, and the other was animal psychologists, and I know we already ...

4.2

a The word *to* is not often stressed. Listen to the first dialogue. Notice the pronunciation /tə/.

b Now practise saying the sentences. Be careful not to stress *to*.

4.3

a Listen again and notice how the intonation goes up when the speaker uses only *Pardon?* or *Sorry?* Practise saying *Pardon?* and *Sorry?* in this way.

b When the speaker uses one of the longer phrases, notice how the intonation goes down on *Sorry?* and also goes down at the end of the sentence. Practise saying these phrases in this way.

4.4

a When a word finishes with a consonant sound, and the next word starts with a vowel sound, the words link together – we say them as if they are one word. Listen to the sentences.

I'm really interested in sports programmes.

I'm not very interested in drama series.

I'm definitely not interested in quiz shows.

b Practise saying the sentences. Try to link the words, where indicated.

4.5

a Cover the tapescript. Fill the gaps with a suitable preposition.

1 It's a thing that mostly men are interested ____ .
2 We can actually get women involved ____ that.
3 ... which I think would appeal ____ all age groups.
4 Men naturally like to look at pretty women ____ television.
5 I was more attracted ____ the programme about hypnosis.

Check with the tapescript.

b Underline the stressed syllable in these words from tapescript 4.5. Then practise saying the words.

particular	programme
interested	presenter
survival	rainforest
camera	natural
hypnosis	psychologist

4.6

Ma Well, er, well, we seem to have one programme that we can all agree on, and that's the one about the Amazon.

Mi You're happy with that, are you?

Ma Yes, I am, I think I could drop the animal psychologist one because ...

Mi You did have two ideas, they were both really sort of about the brain ...

Ma Yes ...

E That'll bring animals in anyway ... from the Amazon.

Ma Exactly, exactly, that's what I thought. (Yeah) So that's, we could go with that one, the survival one and also the point is, it's not expensive (No) as you made that point earlier on, (Right) erm, and let's see if we can agree on the second one. There was the cars.

Mi I'm still very keen on the cars.

Ma Are you? Yeah.

Mi But no, I'm well, you know, I mean I'm happy to change ...

Mi But what about your idea though, for the hypnosis?

Ma Well, I, I'm very keen on that, because we haven't seen anything like that for a while. Again, back to money, it's ... it's not an expensive programme to make, and could be very useful (Yes).

E It's a possibility.

Mi Erm no, I'm, well, I'm happy to go with that.

Ma Are you? Good, right, Eric, what do you think?

E I think we can give it a try, if we make sure that the er, the costs are kept down.

Ma Yes.

Mi OK, great, yep.

Ma Good.

4.7

1 **A** Hello?

   B Oh, hello. Could I speak to David Stone, please?

   A Yep, speaking.

   B Oh, good morning. My name's Angela Green and ...

2 **A** Hello?

   B Oh, oh good afternoon. Is that Mrs Carter?

   A Yes, it is.

   B Oh, hello. My name's Chris Jackson, and ...

3 **A** Hello?

   B Oh, hi, Jim, it's Carrie.

   A Oh, hi, Carrie. How are you?

4.8

AC Hello?

CJ Oh, good afternoon. Is that Mrs Carter?

AC Yes.

CJ My name's Chris Jackson. I'm calling from Alpha Television in Cardiff. Er, I got your name and, erm, number from a colleague of mine (Mmm). Erm, the company's organizing the, er, annual management conference, er, from the first to the third of June (Mmm) and I'm ringing to invite you to give a talk on the use of different interviewing techniques.

AC Oh! Erm, can you just give me the date and time of the talk again, please?

CJ OK, the slot we've got in mind for you would be on the second of June between 10.00 and 11.30.

AC Second of June, 10.00, 11.30 – fine. Erm, how, how long do you want the talk to be?

CJ Well, if we aim for about an hour's talk and then there's some time for questions and answers afterwards.

AC Right.

CJ Erm, the audience will be about 30 managers, who'll be watching you, and the talk's going to take place at the Park Hotel outside Cardiff.

AC Park Hotel, well, I live near Cardiff, so I think I probably know where that is. That's fine.

CJ Erm, can I get down to the nitty gritty? We can offer you a fee of £300 plus expenses.

AC Right, Chris, well, I'd be delighted to accept your offer. That's fine.

CJ That's great.

AC I'll give you my e-mail address so you can confirm – it's acarter@freemail.com

CJ acarterfreemail.com

AC Mhm.

CJ OK, well, I'll get an e-mail off to you with directions and er, well, you probably don't need the map, do you?

AC No, I don't think I do.

CJ You know where it is. OK and if you just acknowledge that you've received that.

AC That's fine.

CJ ... and then we'll look forward to seeing you on the second of June.

4.6

Listen to the conversation, with the tapescript. Underline questions used to ask for an opinion.

Try to use these questions next time you have a conversation in English.

4.6

Look at these words from tapescript 4.6. Notice how we pronounce the letters in bold.

/əʊ/	/ɒ/	/ɔː/	/ʌ/
both	drop	thought	money

Put the words in the box into four groups, according to the pronunciation of the letters in bold.

possibility	love	programme
costs	store	door
not	young	court
home	won	lock
mother	for	go
politics	local	bought
also	some	

4.8

a Look at the tapescript of the telephone conversation between Chris Jackson and Anne Carter. Anne uses *fine, Right, That's fine,* and *Mhm.* Underline all the examples of these words. Why does she use these expressions?

b How do you say these expressions in your language?

5.1

I've got a present for Byron.
Ah, he'll be thrilled.
Who's this for, darling?
Say thank you, Byron.
He's already got that one.
Oh. That's OK, I can change it.
45 quid!!
Oh dear, they've left the price on!
When I think what I could do with £45!
Hey, that's enough, Agrippine.
And here's a little something for you.
Oh, great! Thanks a lot!
£50!
Look, dad, Auntie Mo's given me 50 quid –
that's kind of her, isn't it?
Yeah, but what can you get these days with 50
quid? People are so mean!

5.2

A Why don't you try giving up with a friend?
B Yes, that's a good idea.

A Have you thought about hypnosis?
B Hmm, I'm not sure about that.

A You could avoid places where people smoke.
B Yeah, that sounds sensible.

5.3

It's extremely uncomfortable.
He's unbelievably lazy.
She's got an incredibly good memory.

5.4

Tom

Where I grew up in Sussex, erm, we had these
neighbours, Major and Mrs Wise, very formal
people, very smart people ... he'd just come
out of the army, erm, and some other
neighbours of ours were having a drinks party,
and my father phoned Major and Mrs Wise,
and said, 'You've been asked to this drinks
party, I've been told to phone you, erm, it's a
fancy dress, so please come as whatever you
want, the more outrageous, the better.'
Erm, we all went to this, to this party, and er,
we were standing there and I looked around
and I thought, 'Something's not quite right
here.' Everybody was in suits and ties, the
women were all in dresses, it was a very
formal drinks party.
**Suddenly, there was this knock at the door,
the room went quiet, the door flew open,
there was Major and Mrs Wise. He screamed.
'Me, Tarzan!' and was dressed just as Tarzan,
and she was dressed up just as Jane. It was
horrendous. They never spoke to us again.**

5.5

T You know what happened to me last
  Saturday?
W No, what was that?
T It was terrible. This friend of mine invited
  me to this wedding (Uhuh) of his friends
  (Yeah) and so I assumed it's going to be

very elegant and I went out and bought
this very beautiful dress, very expensive,
(Right) floor length, very long, very
elegant, silk and a huge hat, you can't
imagine, huge elegant hat (Right) and we
arrived there, and everybody's wearing
jeans ...
W Oh, no!!
T ... and shirts in shirtsleeves, and it was
  lovely, it was in the country, and they
  decided they'd have this very relaxed,
  casual wedding, but nobody told me about
  it.
W They hadn't told you.
T I felt like such an idiot, and I couldn't
  change, there was no way I could change
  the situation.
W Still, you've got a long dress and a hat now.
T That's true.

5.6

1 You should leave your trolley over there.
2 You aren't allowed to take the trolley home.
3 You mustn't push in when people are
  queueing.
4 You don't have to make a shopping list.
5 You shouldn't leave your trolley in other
  people's way.

5.7

S Now Janice, I know that this looks like a
  simple job, but erm, there are a few things
  that you should, er, bear in mind. The first
  thing is to keep your eyes open, (Right) er,
  you know, watch out that people don't
  steal chocolate or, you know, magazines,
  whatever, er, because some people do try to
  sort of, er, sneak a few things from the
  shop.
J Right, OK.
S Er, and make sure you check the money
  carefully, the change that you give people.
J Yeah, OK.
S Make sure it's correct, because, you know, it
  costs me money if you make a mistake.
J Yep, OK.
S And er, very important, remember that you
  aren't allowed to sell cigarettes to children.
J Er, do I have to ask children for some
  identity, if I think that they're under 18,
  under 16?
S 16. Oh, yes, absolutely, you know, because
  they do sometimes look bigger and older
  than they are, (Yeah) but it's very
  important, because it's the law of the land,
  so ...
J Oh, and er, is it OK if I help myself to a
  drink or sweets or ... ?
S Er, yes, I mean, within reason. Yes, I
  mean ...
J Oh, great, lovely!
S Yeah, you can have a drink and a you know,
  a piece of chocolate or whatever. Just tell
  me what you've had so that when I come
  to do my stocktaking, I'll know.
J OK, thank you!

5.3

a We usually stress intensifying adverbs, but we also tend to make them longer. Listen to the examples.

b Say the sentences. Remember to make the intensifying adverb longer.

5.4

a Listen again to the part in bold. How does Tom pronounce *was*, *at* and *as*? Practise this part of the recording with your partner.

b We often use *this/these* when we are telling a story or a joke in a very informal way, and we are speaking about someone/something for the first time, for example

I was in this coffee bar, and this man came up to me ...

Circle *this* and *these* in the tapescript. Which of your circled examples mention someone or something for the first time?

5.5

a In her story about the wedding, Trude uses a lot of adjectives. Listen without looking at the tapescript, and try to write down some of the adjectives she uses. Now listen with the tapescript and check your answers.

b What does each adjective refer to? For example, *terrible* refers to the situation.

5.5

Look at these words from tapescript 5.5. Notice how we pronounce the letters in bold.

/ʌ/	/ʊ/	/uː/
c**ou**ntry	c**ou**ld	h**u**ge

Put the words in the box into three groups, according to the pronunciation of the letters in bold.

r**u**de	b**u**tter	p**u**t
m**u**ch	sh**ou**ld	j**u**dge
use	p**u**sh	c**u**pboard
tr**u**e	p**u**dding	b**u**ll
j**ui**ce	s**u**n	

5.7

Look at these words from tapescript 5.7. For each word, underline the stressed syllable.

magazines	carefully
mistake	cigarettes
children	sometimes
important	remember
absolutely	identity

6.1

There's this man called George, right, and he's a salesman in a computer company.

One day, George's boss, the sales manager, is talking to a colleague.

'You know George, he's got an incredibly bad memory,' he says. 'I asked him to buy me some sandwiches at lunchtime, but I'm sure he'll come back to the office without them.'

Suddenly George arrives – very excited – and says, 'You'll never guess what's happened! At lunch I met Fred Brown from the National Bank! We started talking and he agreed to buy one million dollars' worth of computers from us!'

The sales manager then turns to his colleague and says, 'You see? I told you he would forget the sandwiches.'

6.2

A You'll never guess what's happened! I've won $1,000!

B What? You're joking!

A You won't believe who I've just met! Cameron Diaz!

B No, really?

6.3

A So, what's it like then, working in your situation?

C Well, I suppose the main advantage of working in a family business, erm, has to be job security, er, maybe more than in any other working situation ...

A Oh, right, yeah.

C A family business, er, I've come in alongside my father, (I see) erm, we're working together, consequently another advantage is working with people that you know very well. I mean, I've, I've known most of the people here all my life, well, I've grown up, I used to visit my father in the, in the factory ...

A Yes, of course, yeah.

C ... and er, you know, you can, you can almost see and guess how they're going to react ...

A Yes, I can imagine.

C ... knowing them very well, and er, of course, one day, I'll be boss.

A Yeah, absolutely.

C Something I'm looking forward to, and something that worries me too in a way.

A Of course, right.

C There are disadvantages as well.

A Hmm, what are the disadvantages, then?

C Well, I suppose the disadvantage of my situation has to be that other people in the company might not completely trust me because I'm the boss's son.

A Oh, right, yeah.

C You see, in a way, that affects my relationship with them, they assume that I've taken the job or been offered the job because I'm my father's son.

A Hmm, I see.

C Erm, and of course, if you have a problem at work with somebody in the family, it affects your work, and of course you take it home, it affects your family life as well.

A Yes, of course it does.

C But on the whole, I erm, on the whole, I love it. I really feel part of the company and er, yes, I'm enjoying myself, but it's not for everyone.

A No.

6.4

E So, do you like working from home?

M Oh, yes, the great advantage is that I can work when I want to, (Right) and I can stop when I want to eat, and well, eat when I want to, really, it's very good if you have a family and children. (Mm) Erm, also, you don't waste time travelling to and fro from work ...

E Ah, that's very good, yeah.

M ... so you have that extra, extra time, but the main disadvantage is that, well, you don't have that social contact that you get (Hmm) in an office ...

E ... or the friends ... yeah.

M ... or the fellow workers, yeah, erm ... and it's harder to get away from work, it's always, if you've given a part of your house over to it, it's always there, you know, when you pass by the office, you see your computer (Yes, yes). It's harder to escape, and it does take up a lot of room in the house as well.

E Sure.

M That's the main disadvantage.

6.2

a Look at the tapescript. Notice the position of the exclamation marks (!). These are used to indicate surprise.

b Listen to the tapescript again. Notice the energy in the speaker's voice. Say the phrases, copying the rhythm and energy of the speaker's voice.

6.3

a Look at the tapescript. Find the words *advantage* and *disadvantage(s)*.

b How are they pronounced?

c What preposition often follows these words?

d Which words come before *advantage* and *disadvantage(s)*? Now go to the natural English box on page 75.

6.4

The way we say things shows how we feel. How we speak is often as important as the words we use.

a Listen and read at the same time. Notice how Marcella lists the advantages of working at home. She speaks in a clear, direct way.

b Now listen without the tapescript, again paying attention to how Marcella speaks.

6.5

Re Hello, can I help you?

M Er, yes. I'm enquiring about, er, one of the courses. I actually need one that's going to give me a qualification, so do you run courses that lead to diplomas?

Re In what subject exactly?

M Oh, computer studies.

Re Oh, oh yes, we have courses leading to all the best recognized qualifications.

M Oh right, great, OK. Erm, what's the exact length of the course?

Re Er well, we have one which is a nine-month course (Right). That starts on September the 12th, er finishes in June (Nine months). And er, the other one is a one-year course from January to December. It's a bit less intensive.

M OK. The first one you mentioned. What's the starting date for that one?

Re The starting date is the 12th of September.

M 12th, OK, great. Erm, and the weekly timetable. Can you tell me, or give me an example of how that works?

Re Sure. Erm, it's a 15-hour week, usually over about four days, so (15 hours) you usually have one day a week free.

M Oh right, great, OK, erm that's the timetable. The fees. Do I need to give you a deposit of any sort, or ... ?

Re Yes absolutely. The whole course is 1500 but we require a deposit of 300, which we'd like you to send in with the application form.

M OK, that sounds good. Just, er, as a matter of interest, what's the class size for ... for this course?

Re Oh, it's very good actually, about 12–15 students per class.

M Oh, that's good. Yeah OK. Erm ... and what sort of requirements do you need for, you know, for entry? You know, what sort of qualifications do I need to have?

Re Well, if you have school qualifications (Yep) and basic computer skills (OK), you should be fine.

M OK, great. Erm, and last question was, how do I enrol? What do I need to do now?

Re Well er, do you have an application form?

M Yep.

Re Right. Well, if you fill that in and send it in with your deposit (OK), and er, when the course starts, you pay the rest of the fees.

M Great. OK, I think that's everything I need. Erm ... thanks very much for your help.

Re OK, pleasure. Bye bye.

M OK, bye bye.

6.6

C So Andrew, what have you and Rowena decided to do in the end?

A Oh, well, you, you know, so we've been er, we've been talking about this for ages. I told you the options we were discussing, (yeah) the photography, me starting my own business ...

C Yes, that sounded like a good idea.

A Well, it sounded like a good idea but actually it's far too risky. I don't really know how to run my own business, and er, it would be expensive to set up (Sure) and I haven't really got the experience, I don't think.

C No, that's true.

A Hmm. So then there was the option of erm, staying at home, me staying at home ...

C Yes, looking after the baby.

A ... hmm, while Rowena carried on working. Erm, neither of us are really happy with that. (Hmm) No, I would like to carry on working, and strangely enough, Rowena wants to stop.

C Yeah, well that's understandable, yeah.

A Yeah? She wants to be at home and look after the baby (Mm) so erm, so that's not really going to work, I don't think. (Hmm) And then there was the idea of moving somewhere else where I would be able to get the same sort of job as I've got at the moment (Yes). Erm, no! (No) We really don't want to because all our family ...

C Your family, exactly.

A ... absolutely, we're all here in this area, all our friends, we know the area and so, erm, no we don't want to move.

C No, stay put.

A Yep. And then finally there's retraining, me retraining, er, in a different area. Well, business management is what we've set on because (Right) there's a course at the local college (Excellent) that I can do, only takes a year, (Yeah) and then there are lots of, er, chances of me getting work in that area (Mhm). It will mean that money will be tight for a while, (Mm) but erm, there won't be much money, but I'll get a small grant so erm, that's what we've decided to go for. (Good) I'm going to retrain.

C Oh, that sounds great.

A I'm going to be a student again.

6.5

When we have a conversation, we often need time to think about what we are going to say. To give ourselves time to think, we can repeat certain sounds or words.

Look at the tapescript. Underline words the speakers use to give themselves time to think, for example *Er* ... .

Check your answers with the answer key.

6.5

Notice the sound /ɜ:/ in the word *work*. When vowels are placed next to the letter *r* they are sometimes pronounced /ɜ:/. Look at these examples

heard (e+a+r)

university (e+r)

first (i+r)

work (o+r)

nurse (u+r)

Guess the words by reading the definitions. All of the words have the sound /ɜ:/ in them.

1 Twenty-first, twenty-second, _ _ _ _ _ _ - _ _ _ _ _
2 We always eat _ _ _ _ _ _ for Christmas lunch, never chicken.
3 He's travelled all over the _ _ _ _ _ .
4 It's not his, it's _ _ _ _.
5 What's your salary? How much do you _ _ _ _ ?
6 Is Andrea a boy's name or a _ _ _ _ '_ name?
7 I'm going to be away for three days – Tuesday, Wednesday, and _ _ _ _ _ _ _ _ .
8 Do you find it easy to _ _ _ _ _ languages?
9 'Can you help me please?' '_ _ _ _ _ _ _ _ _ . What's the matter?'
10 'Can I borrow your dictionary? I need to look up this _ _ _ _ .'

seven

7.1

I don't know what you see in that idiot, Trevor.

He's great.

No he's not. He's awful.

You don't know the first thing about it. I'm good at choosing men.

And he's got a big bum.

Look, you have to think about the future – OK, he's a bit fat now, but at 18 he'll be gorgeous.

Sorry, but his clothes are dreadful.

You know everyone's saying you've fallen in love with him.

Well, I wouldn't tell you anyway – you're just a gossip.

Have you kissed him yet?

I'm not telling you.

So what do you do when you go out?

Well, we have a good time. I don't understand everything he says but you wouldn't understand a single word.

So when are you going to finish with him, then?

How can you be so rude and tactless?

Ask me another ...

7.2

Conversation 1

... I didn't agree with everything but, erm ... no, no, he did. Look, as we're talking about work, erm Angela, there's, there's something I've been meaning to say, (Hmm) er, it's only a small thing, but er, it's just that, when we're at work and I'm really trying to concentrate, erm, if you, if you interrupt me, I just lose my train of thought completely, erm (Oh!) it's like today, when you came over ...

Conversation 2

D You look worried. Are you OK?

A No, I, I ... I'm fine. Erm, er, Dave, erm, I do want to talk to you about something, though, that's erm, (Mm) that's been on my mind er, recently. Erm, it's quite difficult for me to say, really.

D No, go on, if you've got something to say, I'd rather you were honest and just said it.

A Right. Erm, the thing is, I, I like you, I like you very much, you know that, we're very good friends, erm but I, I ... don't really think that we have a lot in common (Hmm) really, and er, in terms of going out together as boyfriend and girlfriend, I, I'm ... I ... I really don't want to do that any more, to be honest with you. I ... I'll be very happy to go out with you as just friends, but erm, I'm, I ...

D Are you saying it's over?

A Not, not our friendship, but just in terms of (But yes) boyfriend and girlfriend ...

D ... going out with (Yes) ... it's over.

A Yes.

D Well, if it's me, if it's because of the way ... I can change. I mean, if it's something about me that you don't like, tell me what it is ...

A No, no, it's not ...

D ... and I'll change that.

A It's not that I don't like, I do like you, that's why I'd like us still to be friends. (Hmm) I do like you but I think we haven't really got that much in common. I mean, our friends are very different kinds of people. I find your friends erm, well ... it's just that we haven't got a lot in common. (Hmm) That's what I mean.

D OK.

7.3

A Mmm!

B Is it OK? It's not too strong?

A No, it's perfect.

B Great. Erm, actually, Carole, there's something I wanted to ask you.

A Hmm?

B I mean, I hope you don't mind, and you can say no if you want, it's, it's no problem, honestly.

A Oh, dear, I don't like the sound of this!

B No, it's not that bad, honestly! (Right) You see, the thing is, I was wondering if you could give me a hand, you see. Well, I've got to write this essay, and I just don't know the subject well enough, and it's got to be in by Monday.

A OK, well, look – no problem – tell me, what, what is the subject?

B I've been putting it off for ages. It's about the traffic situation in central London.

A Oh, and you don't drive!

B Well, I don't live in London!

7.4

I **do** feel sorry for that little child.

I like him and he really **does** work hard.

I **did** enjoy the film; it was brilliant!

I'm sure I **did** pay that bill.

7.2

a Look at the beginning of the conversations. Underline the phrases that Jonathan and Ann use to prepare the listener for bad news.

Do you think the speakers are very direct or not?

b Look at the dictionary extract for *really*. Match the underlined examples with the correct definition.

> really /'rɪəli/ **adv** **1** actually; in fact: *I couldn't believe it was really happening.* • *He said he was sorry but I don't think he really meant it.* • *She wasn't really angry, she was only pretending.* • *Is it really true?* **2** very; very much: *I'm really tired.* • *Are you really sure?* • *I really hope you enjoy yourself.* • *I really tried but I couldn't do it.* **3** used as a question for expressing surprise, interest, doubt, etc: *'She's left her husband.' 'Really? When did that happen?'* **4** used in negative sentences to make what you are saying less strong: *I don't really agree with that.*
>
> entry from *Oxford Wordpower Dictionary*
> ISBN 0194315169

7.3

a Look at these phrases from the first part of the tapescript. We can use these before we ask somebody to do something difficult for us.

… there's <u>some</u>thing I <u>want</u>ed to <u>ask</u> you.

I <u>hope</u> you don't <u>mind</u> …

… you <u>can</u> say <u>no</u> if you <u>want</u> …

b Listen to the cassette. Notice the stress and intonation.

c Practise saying these phrases. Try to use them the next time you ask somebody to do something for you.

7.5

I   So, Joe, how did your evening go?

J   Er, it was great. I erm, I chose a place that was near where I live, well, er, ten or twenty minutes' walk, but er, I was late, so erm, I had to take a taxi, and that cost er, roughly £3.

I   Right, OK, and erm, did you buy anything to wear for the date?

J   Me? No, I'm not bothered about my appearance, no. I didn't buy any clothes, I didn't get my hair cut, no, nothing. Anyway, erm, we arranged to meet for a drink before going to the restaurant (Oh, right) and er, well I felt relaxed, (Yes) and she arrived about five minutes after me and I offered to buy her a drink, well, we were, we were going to go halves, but erm, the man is expected, I think, to buy, to buy the first drink (OK). So anyway, we, erm, we went to the restaurant, and erm, well we both had quite a lot to eat, and a decent bottle of wine or two!

I   Great! And erm, who, er, who paid for the meal?

J   Erm, when the bill came, erm, I offered to pay, well she said no. Erm, I bought drinks after dinner, I tipped the waiter, and erm, the meal cost me about £25, well, more or less, I think, and the whole evening was £46, something like that anyway, which erm, I thought was quite reasonable. We had a great evening anyway.

I   Great – thank you.

7.6

Story 1

L   Well, my favourite film ever is, er, is about a relationship. Er, **a man and a woman meet in a railway restaurant (Oh, yeah) because she has something in her eye, and he's a doctor, so he comes forward and helps her to get this out of her eye, and er, they meet several times after that, and eventually realize that they are falling in love with each other,** but the problem is that they are both married to other people. (Oh, no!) And er, then one day she comes home very late from having met this man and her children are both very ill, so she feels terribly guilty about this. She thinks that somehow she's responsible for her children being ill, because she's been having a relationship with this man, (Oh!) and she realizes it's going to have to stop. But, well they're very involved with each other by this time, and she doesn't want to stop it, but eventually of course, it has to come to an end, and he goes off to Africa, I think, to be a heroic doctor in Africa, (Really?) and she goes back to her children and her husband, and it's all terribly sad and moving.

F   Oh, that's so sad!

Story 2

This is a film, and it's about this kind of cute, shy guy who runs a bookshop (Hmm) and one day, this incredibly famous, glamorous American actress, movie star comes in and, and she buys a couple of books, but erm, you know, nothing else happens. (Ah) But a bit later, they bump into each other again, and they start to spend time together and you realize then that, that they're falling in love, oh, it's so sweet. Anyway, after that, they meet on a few occasions, but each time, something goes wrong. Now, they're in love, but they keep having arguments, basically because she's so famous, and he's not, (Yeah, yeah) and they live in different worlds (Right, right). In the end, he realizes that it's now or never, and what he does is he interrupts a press conference that she's giving, and he says that he loves her, and it has a happy ending. At the end of the film, they get married and they have a baby.

7.7

It was very silly.
It made me laugh.
I found it very moving.

7.6

a Read the first story again. Underline all the examples of verbs in the present simple.

b Now look only at the present simple verbs which end in *s*. Put them into the following groups

1 verbs that end in the sound /s/ (e.g. *stops*)
2 verbs that end in the sound /z/ (e.g. *lives*)
3 verbs that end in the sound /ɪz/ (e.g. *washes*)

Check with the answer key.

7.6

Notice the pronunciation of the word *wear* /weə/ in tapescript 7.6. When two vowels are placed next to the letter *r* they are sometimes pronounced /eə/. Look at these examples.

pear (e+a+r)

care (a+r+e)

hair (a+i+r)

there (e+r+e)

their (e+i+r)

All the words in the box have the sound /eə/ in them. Find pairs of words that have the same pronunciation.

pair	stair	fair
there	air	where
bare	fare	bear
stare	their	heir
pear	wear	

7.7

a Listen without the tapescript. Count the number of words in each sentence.

b Listen again and write the sentences. Check your answers with the tapescript.

8.1

There's a businessman, sitting in an airport lounge, and he's waiting for a very important client to arrive, and he looks across the lounge, and he sees Bill Gates sitting alone on the other side of the lounge. So he goes over to him and he introduces himself and he says, 'Mr Gates, my client is a really, really big fan of yours. Could you do me a favour? You see, I'm waiting for him, and when he arrives, do you think you could walk past me, and just tap me on the shoulder and say, 'Hi, John! How are you doing?' and Bill Gates says, 'Yeah, sure.'

So, erm, the client arrives, and Bill Gates sees him arrive and he comes across, and he taps John on the shoulder and says, 'Hi, John!' and John turns round to Bill and says, 'Oh, go away, Bill! Can't you see I'm busy?'

8.2

A Could you do me a favour?
B Of course. What is it?

A Could you give me a hand?
B Sure.

A Could you do something for me?
B It depends what it is.

8.3

C Hello, 2949?
D Hi, is that Colin?
C Yup.
D It's Diana here.
C Hi! How are you?
D I'm really well, how are you?
C Very well, thanks.
D Good, so anyway, I was wondering if you'd like to come over for dinner sometime next week.
C Oh, Diana, I'd love to, but I can't. I'm going abroad.
D Are you?
C Yeah.
D (Really?) Where are you going?
C Well, it's happened really quickly but I'm going to Kazakhstan.
D (Kazakhstan!)
C Yes!
D My goodness! Well, what exactly are you going to do out there?
C Well, you know that oil company I got, erm, I started working for last year ...
D Mmm ...
C Well, this opportunity came up in Kazakhstan, and the money's terrific, and I thought, it's just too good an opportunity to miss.
D Wow, that sounds exciting. When are you going?
C Next Friday!
D Next Friday!
C So I've got so much preparation to do

before then that I really can't commit myself to anything, I'm afraid.
D No, well, I can understand that. How long are you going for?
C Well, initially, I'm going for a month, erm, but then one month out there and one month back, for possibly a year, or maybe even two years.
D Hey, that's great. Whereabouts are you staying?
C Well, I'm staying in a hotel to start with, it's all been arranged, but what I'm hoping to do on my second visit is look around for a flat or an apartment or something (yeah) because I hate hotels. It'll be OK for the first few weeks, you know, but I'd rather have somewhere that I can just, you know, settle in, and call home.
D Yes, of course, I understand, and gosh, Kazakhstan! So, are you going to do any travelling while you're there?
C Well, I hope so.

8.4

D Yes, of course, I understand, and gosh, Kazakhstan! So, are you going to do any travelling while you're there?
C Well, I hope so. I mean, I really don't know anything about the place at all – so I'll see when I get there, I suppose.
D Do you know what language they speak there?
C I haven't even got a clue! Listen, if it works out, come out and visit?
D Oh, I'd love to! I bet that would be a really interesting place to visit.
C Well, I tell you what, I'll talk to you next month when I get back, and er, maybe I'll have sorted out somewhere to stay then ...
D Fantastic!
C ... and er, I'll give you a call.
D Yeah, do that!
C All right. Well, listen, I'll see you soon. I'm sorry about next week.
D That's OK, not to worry, I'll see you hopefully in Kazakhstan!
C Yeah, I'll send you a card.
D OK, bye!
C Bye!

8.5

How long are you going for?
Who are you working with?
What are you so angry about?

8.2

a Listen to the examples. Notice how *could* is pronounced.

b Listen again. In the questions, which words are stressed?

c Practise saying the questions, paying attention to the stress and the pronunciation of *could*. See how fast you can say them!

8.3

a Look at Diana's questions which have been underlined.

How does she pronounce *are*?

Listen again.

Practise saying the questions.

b Look at Diana's responses. She responds to Colin's news with surprise and excitement. Circle the phrases she uses, as in the examples.

Practise saying the phrases.

8.6

1 to express pleasure: *Ah! Great! Ooh! Wow!*
2 to express surprise: *What? Oh!*
3 to express pain: *Ow! Ouch!*
4 to express anger: *Oh no!*
5 when something bad has happened: *Oh no! Oh dear!*

8.7

1 **A** Could I borrow the iron, please?
  B Yes, sure.
2 **A** Do you mind if I use the washing machine?
  B No, that's fine.
3 **A** Do you think I could make a phone call?
  B Yes you can, as long as it's quick. I'm expecting a call.
4 **A** Would you mind if I cooked something for myself?
  B No, of course not – go ahead.

8.8

T Hello, Mrs Clark.
Mrs C Oh hi, Trude.
T Erm, I've got to tell you something, I just dropped a glass in my bedroom ...
Mrs C Oh, dear!
T ... and it actually broke.
Mrs C Oh!
T I'm very sorry!
Mrs C Did you cut yourself?
T No, I didn't, no, erm, but I'm going to replace it.
Mrs C Oh, Trude, don't worry about it. It's just a glass. Forget about it.
T Oh, thank you very much. **Er, Mrs Clark, I wanted to ask you, do you have a computer in the house?**
Mrs C **Well, we do, actually. It's, it's over there, in that room.**
T **And are you on the Internet?**
Mrs C **We are, because my husband, you see, has his own business, ...**
T **Yeah.**
Mrs C **... and he works from home a lot, so he needs his computer, he uses it a lot.**
T **Oh, that's great. Do you think I could use it? I'd like to check, er, if I have any e-mail messages. And also, I would love to send a message to my family back home, to tell them that I've arrived all right.**
Mrs C **Oh, of course, you must send them a message right away.**
T Oh, that's fantastic. Thank you very much.
Mrs C Oh, and Trude, I wanted to ask you – we usually have breakfast before nine o'clock – is there anything you don't eat? Are you a vegetarian or anything?

T No.
Mrs C What do you normally eat for breakfast?
T I like coffee in the morning, and perhaps a bit of bread, or a roll or something – really simple.
Mrs C And that's enough?
T Yes.
Mrs C OK, and normally what I do is, I have cereal and juice and fruit is out, and you just help yourself to that whenever you like.
T Oh, that's lovely!
Mrs C OK.
T Thank you very much, Mrs Clark.
Mrs C It's my pleasure. You have a nice day today.
T Thank you. You too!

8.7

a Notice the words with the main stress.

Could I <u>borrow</u> the <u>iron</u>, <u>please</u>?

Do you <u>mind</u> if I <u>use</u> the <u>washing</u> <u>machine</u>?

Do you <u>think</u> I could <u>make</u> a <u>phone</u> call?

Would you <u>mind</u> if I <u>cooked</u> something for <u>myself</u>?

b Practise saying the questions, paying attention to the stress.

8.8

Cover the tapescript. Look at the text below, and fill each gap with a suitable word.

T   Hello, Mrs Clark.

Mrs C Oh hi, Trude.

T   Erm, I've got to tell you something, I just ¹ _____ a glass in my bedroom ...

Mrs C Oh, dear!

T   ... and it actually broke.

Mrs C Oh!

T   I'm very sorry!

Mrs C Did you ² _____ yourself?

T   No, I didn't, no, erm, but I'm going to replace it.

Mrs C Oh, Trude, don't ³ _____ about it. It's just a glass. Forget about it.

T   Oh, thank you very much. Er, Mrs Clark, I ⁴ _____ to ask you, do you have a computer in the house?

Mrs C Well, we do, actually. It's, it's over there, in that room.

T   And are you ⁵ _____ the Internet?

Mrs C We are, because my husband, you see, has his own business, ...

T   Yeah.

Mrs C ... and he works from home a lot, so he needs his computer, he uses it a lot.

T   Oh, that's great. Do you think I could use it? I'd like to ⁶ _____, er, if I have any e-mail messages. And also, I would love to ⁷ _____ a message to my family back home, to tell them that I've arrived all right.

Mrs C Oh, of course, you must send them a message ⁸ _____ away. Oh, and Trude, I wanted to ask you – we usually have breakfast before nine o'clock, is there anything you don't eat? Are you a ⁹ _____ or anything?

T   No.

Mrs C What do you normally eat for breakfast?

T   I like coffee in the morning, and perhaps a bit of bread, or a roll or something – really simple.

Mrs C And that's enough?

T   Yes.

Mrs C OK, and normally what I do is, I have cereal and juice and fruit is out, and you just ¹⁰ _____ _____ to that whenever you like.

T   Oh, that's lovely!

Mrs C OK.

T   Thank you very much, Mrs Clark.

Mrs C It's my pleasure. You have a nice day today.

T   Thank you. You too!

Check your answers with the tapescript.

8.8

Look at this phrase from tapescript 8.8.

... is there anything you don't eat?

In English the letters *th* can be pronounced like in the word *there* /ð/ or like in the word *anything* /θ/.

Put the words in the box into two groups, according to the pronunciation of the letters *th*.

/ð/	/θ/
together	three

this	thirty	thin
those	mother	both
healthy	then	thick
there	thirsty	with
teeth	these	

9.1

Mum, I'm taking some chicken from the fridge
... and I'll need 30 quid, OK?
NO!

There's a barbecue at the beach tonight.
You aren't expecting me to drive you, I hope.
Of course not – we're hitching there with
Angostura and her boyfriend.
So, how are you getting back?

Don't worry – at 11.00 on the dot we're
meeting Noel's dad on his way home from his
poker game, and he'll drop us at a café where
Sebastian will pick us up.

He'll drop us at Nick's, and then Nick'll bring
us home if he's got the car.

If not, we'll walk to the village and get the
old man there to take us on his tractor to the
all-night café where we know some boys with
motorbikes and they'll give us a lift home.

OK, OK, I'll drive you.
Well, only if it makes you happy.

9.2

1 DeNica

If I have to buy a present for someone,
erm, I really like to take my time. I spend
a lot of time choosing the right gift, I'll
go into many different shops, before I've
really found that special present for the
person that I'm thinking of, to give them
on their birthday.

2 Tyler

I have a very high-powered job, so during
the week, I have lunch in a hurry. I can't
hang around, I've got to move on. If I
had more time, like on holiday, for
example, I'd have a very long, slow, lazy
lunch.

3 Julia

I spend ages tidying up. It, it's
impossible, really. I work from home and
there's papers all over the place. If I had
a cleaner, things'd be different and the
place might just get tidy quicker.

4 Patience

I always seem to be in a hurry in the
morning. It doesn't mean I haven't got up
early but I just never seem to have
enough time, so I always do everything as
quickly as possible, like have breakfast. I
quickly pour on a bit of milk on to my
muesli and eat it standing up while I'm
trying to put some clothes on at the
same.

9.3

Jeff

I hate to be in a rush when I'm taking a
bath. I like to take my time over it, I read a
book, I let the water get cool and then warm
it up again, and oh, really until my fingers
begin to look like prunes.

Ralph

Breakfast for me is a ritual. I spend ages
having my breakfast, having my muesli, my
toast, my cup of tea, and it's, er, I, I need
that time every day to just gather my
thoughts, and if I miss out on any one of
those things, then I feel that my day is off
to a bad start. I even wake up looking
forward to my breakfast. I love it!

9.4

A How long would it take you to do that
exercise?

B It would take about half an hour.

A Does it take long to get there?

B No, not very long.

9.2

Look at the tapescript. Underline the sentences which begin *If I had …*

You are going to study this now. Go to page 107 in the student's book.

9.3

Cover the tapescript. Listen to Ralph talking about his breakfast and complete the text below. Listen again, if necessary.

Breakfast for me is a ritual. I spend [1] _____ having my breakfast, having my muesli, my [2] _____ , my [3] _____ _____ _____ , and it's, er, I, I [4] _____ that time every [5] _____ to just gather my thoughts, and if I [6] _____ out on any one of those things, then I feel that my [7] _____ is off to a bad start. I even [8] _____ up looking forward to my breakfast. I love it!

Check your answers with the tapescript.

9.4

a Listen to the cassette. Notice how the words are linked together in groups (/). This always happens in spoken English.

  A How long / would it take you / to do that exercise?
  B It would take about / half an hour.
  A Does it take long / to get there?
  B No, not very long.

b Practise saying the sentences, first with and then without the tapescript.

9.5

A Do you find your English students get much of a chance to practise their English outside of the classroom?

J Well, yes, erm, they very often go to the cinema, erm, we've got a couple of cinemas in, in town that will show films in the original language, in English, erm, once a week, and er, now and again I think some of them watch satellite TV too.

A Oh, that's good.

J And of course, they can rent videos, and I think videos are very good because students can watch bits again and again if they don't understand something (Oh yes) then obviously they can go back and listen, erm, and of course, they listen to music all the time, (Of course) and I suppose occasionally some of them might read the words as they're listening ...

A Read along with (Possibly) the words of the song.

A Yes, and I suppose they use the Internet, do they?

J I think they do, erm yeah, quite a lot. They know how to do e-mails and, and probably circulate little jokes and stories amongst themselves. (Of course, yes) Some of them have er, cyberfriends, for example, or they might have some kind of group where they communicate with each other on e-mail, erm, and actually I think quite often some of them go up to the bigger language schools as well, and there might be talks or events in English, and yes, my students will occasionally go to those.

A I see, and, and, and what about speaking English? Do they get much of a chance?

J Mm, yes, that's difficult but erm, one class has set up a ... a kind of club where they meet together in a bar, oh, maybe once a week or so, (Yes) and perhaps they'll invite English speakers to come in and and start off some sort of conversation or discussion, or just generally so that they can practise their English. (Oh, I see) So it's quite good (Yes).

9.5

Cover the tapescript. Complete the text below, using the phrases in the box.

rent videos	satellite TV
now and again	show films
go to the cinema	in English
again and again	a couple of

A Do you find your English students get much of a chance to practise their English outside of the classroom?

J Well, yes, erm, they very often
1 _____ , erm, we've got
2 _____ cinemas in town
that will 3 _____ in the
original language,
4 _____ , erm, once a
week, and er, 5 _____ I
think some of them watch
6 _____ too.

A Oh, that's good.

J And of course, they can
7 _____ , and I think
videos are very good because students
can watch bits 8 _____ if
they don't understand something ...

Check your answers with the tapescript.

9.5

The *s* at the end of plural nouns is sometimes pronounced /s/ (e.g. *students, bits, jokes, talks, events*), and is sometimes pronounced /z/ (e.g. *cinemas, films, videos, words, e-mails, stories, cyberfriends, schools, speakers*).

Put the words in the box into two groups, according to the pronunciation of the letter *s*.

/s/	/z/
hats	chairs

chairs	hats	pens
books	magazines	mountains
chips	forks	lips
toys	clouds	biscuits
windows	tights	

10.1

There are three women, and they're having coffee together, and they're boasting about their sons. So the first woman says, 'Oh, I've got the most wonderful son. Do you know that last year for my birthday, he gave a big party for me at an expensive restaurant?' The wo... second woman says. 'Oh, really? Well, my son, last winter, paid for me to go on a luxury cruise around the world. First class!' And the third woman says, 'That's nothing! My son's been going to a psychiatrist three times a week for five years at $80 an hour. And he spends the whole time talking about me!'

10.2

I think parents tend to worry too much about their teenage children.
On the whole, parents are stricter with their first child than with later children.

10.3

Story 1

I only ever had one teenage birthday party at my house, when I was ... a teenager, and er my, er my mum and dad insisted on staying in the house (Mmm). It wasn't a very big house. And er, things were going alright – it was quite a good party – but er, I was worried 'cos the music was too loud and things were getting a bit noisy. And then at 11 o'clock, my father appeared in his pyjamas (Oh) winding an alarm clock, er which everybody took as a signal to leave. I've never (Oh) been so embarrassed (Ah).

Story 2

R I had a party when I was about er, 15, 16, and erm, I'd actually, I'd actually forgotten about it until recently, when I was looking back at some photos. (Mm) Er, it was my birthday party, but I looked at the photo and I realized that I was the only boy at my own 15th birthday party, and I said to Mum, I said, I said, 'I can't actually remember the party Mum, why, why were there no boys in, in this picture?' (She said), 'Well there were no boys at the party.'

M What?

R I said, 'Why?' She said, 'Well you didn't really have many friends so we had to ask all your sister's friends instead.' It was unbel ... I couldn't believe it.

M What was that like then?

R Well, I can't remember, but I mean it'd be fantastic now.

M Yeah!

10.4

Marcella

Just thinking about when I was at school, and my primary school teachers, they were on the whole very caring. (Hmm) That was, that's my memory of it, sort of gentle people, really. I mean, I know that you get the odd teacher who's ... could be bad-tempered or whatever (Oh, yeah) but er, <u>my memory of them</u> is that they were, yeah, very caring people. It must be because when you're very young, you're so open as a child, and maybe the response is, you know, you know, the way children are so open, <u>the response is to just look after them</u>, (Yeah) rather than anything else (Hmm).

Michael

Mi Don't you find, generally speaking, that er, people who present chat shows are just so fake?

Ma Oh, absolutely!

Mi And they, they, they, they're only really interested in asking questions, (Mm) and they're never really interested in what people answer. (Mm) I think so, they ask a question, and then <u>while the person's talking to them</u>, they look down at their, their piece of paper and try and find out what their next question's going to be. (Mm) And the really good ones actually listen and have a conversation with people, (Yes) but actually most of them, are useless, I think.

Ma Ego!

Mi Hm.

Gareth

University students – they've got this terrible reputation. People assume that they're lazy, that they don't do any work, that they just, er, you know, muddle their way through their exams, that they live in a complete mess, and in my experience, that's not true. (Really?) The students that I come across, they work hard, they're at least as tidy as I am, and mostly they just want to get on with their work and get a decent job at the end of it (Hmm!).

10.4

a Listen again to the first two conversations. How is the word *them* pronounced? Practise saying the underlined phrases.

b Complete the phrases with a preposition.

1 ___ the whole, they're very caring.
2 They live ___ a complete mess.
3 ___ my experience, that's not true.
4 They're ___ least as tidy as me.
5 They're only interested ___ asking questions.

Check with the tapescript.

ten

10.5

DeNica

I suppose the thing I think about, er, in terms of a female rock star would be the entourage that er, she has following her, all the millions of helpers, the dietician, the gym trainer, the designer, the vocal coach, erm, I, I imagine that they live a very isolated life, actually, erm, like Madonna, erm, has to in America, you know ...

Jonathan

J Well, I think the stereotypes of rock stars have changed, you know, I mean er, in the sixties and seventies it was hard drinking, hard living, you know, late nights, er, (Yeah) lots of girlfriends and now, it seems, er, they've got people like Westlife and Ronan Keating, very clean cut, (Yeah that's true) very, er, clean living, married, settled down, erm, which is really, really nice but, erm ... bit boring.

D Not as glamorous.

J No.

10.6

Do you fancy going out for a meal tonight?
How about coming over for a drink this evening?
I was wondering if you'd like to see a film.

10.7

Part 1

A I am so sorry!

M Hello!

A How lovely to see you!

M Lovely to see you! Are you all right?

A Oh, fine. I got horribly stuck in traffic on the way in, absolutely terrible, and, and there's nowhere to park round here, is there?

M I know, I know, it's terrible. I've had to park miles away.

A Well, I'm about, about five streets away, actually, I think. So, and I ... I'm on a meter which I'll possibly have to check ...

M Forget it, just let's, let's just forget it.

A Forget it! All right.

W Good evening.

A/M Hello.

W Can I get you a drink?

A Er, what are you having?

M Erm, I've just got a, a glass of wine here.

A I ... no, I'm driving back. I think I'll, erm, I'll have an orange juice.

W Just an orange juice ...

Part 2

A Oh, actually, before I forget, 'cos I know I'll go through the whole evening ... I'm going to a really lovely dinner at the Sheraton Hotel ...

M Mm, very nice!

A Next Saturday evening, like, like you do, and I'd like you to come.

M Oh, Alison!

A ... if that's all right.

M To the Sheraton?

A Yes. It's paid for, and everything, it's sort of a works do.

M Aah ...

A What? No ...

M Oh, dear, you said, it's not this Saturday?

A Yes, oh, please, come on, it'll, it'll be fun!

M Er, look I ... I'd love to, (Right) but unfortunately, I've got, I've got to prepare a presentation for work, it's, it's for, for Monday, 150 people. Erm ...

A Well, you could leave your work till Sunday, and work really hard on Sunday.

M I'm afraid my stepson's coming over on Sunday, it's, er, it's one of these weekends ... oh what a shame, I'd love to have ...

10.8

Jo I think there's been a change about how people use the phone. I think in the past, women spent more time on the phone, but now, I think men do, and I'll tell you what it is – I think it's mobile phones, because men love walking around town thinking they're busy, on the mobile phoning lots of people, and I bet if you added that time up, men would spend longer on the phone than women.

Ju But, can I just say that the conversations are not as long, so if we're talking how much time people spend on the phone, women definitely spend longer on the phone than men because they have long chats, long conversations.

Jo I agree in one conversation, but I bet if you added up ...

10.5

Listen to the pronunciation of these words from tapescript 10.5.

/ʃ/	/tʃ/	/dʒ/
dietician	coach	gym

Look at these examples.

1 words with the sound /ʃ/

machine, election, shoes, washing, sugar

2 words with the sound /tʃ/

furniture, research, chips, church, picture

3 words with the sound /dʒ/

message, judge, generally, juice, gin

Which group does each word belong to? Write 1, 2, or 3 next to each word.

☐1	shirt	☐	bridge
☐	cheap	☐	chef
☐	cheque	☐	jump
☐	chocolate	☐	joke
☐	ashtray	☐	jazz
☐	architecture	☐	station
☐	garage	☐	British
☐	chicken		

10.6

a Listen to the sentences. Underline the stressed words in the tapescript. Then check your answers with the answer key.

b Practise saying the sentences, paying attention to the stress.

10.7

a Look at the tapescript for part 1 of the conversation between Alison and Max. They do three different things during their conversation.

1 they greet each other
2 they give and accept reasons for being late
3 they order a drink

Mark the three different parts of their conversation on the tapescript.

b When people have a conversation, both speakers often use similar words. This helps to keep the conversation moving, for example

A This machine's **broken**.
B **Broken**? Really?

Look at the part of Alison and Max's conversation where they talk about the traffic. Find three examples of this kind of repetition.

Next time you have a conversation in English, try to use repetition like this.

10.8

a Find these common conversational phrases in the tapescript.

1 ... I'll tell you what it is
2 ... I bet ...
3 ... can I just say ...

b How do you say these in your language?

11.1

Oh no! I look horrendous. It doesn't look like me at all.

Yeah, and I'm sure that's not me.

Do you really think it's us?

Hmm ... that's your jacket, isn't it?

I think someone must have been in there before us with the same jacket on as me.

Yeah, could be, and the other one had the same polo neck as me.

Honestly, it's so annoying that some girl is going about dressed like me.

You can say that again ... let's get changed and do the photos again.

11.2

My friend, Patric, was born in a village in Switzerland in the 1970s, but he grew up in Zurich. He was educated at an ordinary state college, and went on to university to study economics. When he left, he was offered a job in a bank, but he decided to travel round the world. When he came back, he wrote a book about his experiences. It has been translated into four languages and is now sold in 30 different countries.

11.3
Elly

Well, I was born in Canada, in Toronto, er, as an only child, erm, and it wasn't until I was three years old that we moved to England, me and my parents, erm. They had quite lot of money, they were quite wealthy, they had their, erm, their own furniture business. Erm, I started school, did pretty well, eight GCSEs, erm, and went to college and then went on to university, where I studied economics.

Well, my father initially wanted me to join the family furniture business, which was natural I suppose, erm, but I wasn't really into it. Anyway I did work there for two years and actually hated every minute of it and after those two years I, I started to realize that what I really wanted to do was to become an actress, erm, which my parents weren't too keen on, but I was. So I went to drama school for three years which was fantastic, er, I had the best time of my life there, made so many good friends, and that's where I met Tom, my husband.

Erm, it wasn't until, sort of mid thirties that I did get my big break. Erm, I got a part in, erm, a soap opera on TV, erm, and worked in there for two to three years and became a household name. I had some quite big story lines and stuff, which was nice. Er, I left the soap opera and, erm, because I was well known by then, I started to get film parts, and I did that for a few years, but eventually I found that I got a bit tired of the fame and the recognition, and in my mid fifties I decided to retire, my husband did as well, and erm, we actually moved to a Mediterranean island, er, so we lived there, grew our own food, kept goats and chickens and pigs and cows, and all that, which was really nice and basically had a very quiet life, for once.

11.4

E   Then, erm, complete surprise, completely out of the blue, two years ago, my agent phoned me and I was offered a part in a major Hollywood movie, erm, which was a real shock to me, because I hadn't worked for so long, but Tom persuaded me in the end that I should do it, erm, which in the end was the right decision, because I worked with the most fantastic director, erm, and the film was a big success all over the world. And then, another turn up for the books, erm, I won, erm, an Oscar for Best Actress at 70 – which was amazing!

I   So, er, do you think that was your greatest achievement?

E   Erm, well, yes!

11.5

I was hoping to work in television, but in the end, I got a job in radio.

I was planning to travel a lot, but I ended up getting married and settling down.

11.6

Sir Ludovic Kennedy was born into a wealthy English family and had two younger sisters. He went to the famous public school, Eton, and towards the end of his time there, in 1938, he decided to charter a plane, together with four other friends, and fly to France and back in a day. Amazingly, it only cost £3 each at the time, and they managed to do it without the school finding out.

He then went on to Oxford University, but his studies were interrupted when war broke out the following year. He joined the Navy, where he had a distinguished career. After the war, he finished his degree, and was then offered a job in television, first as a newscaster and later as a political journalist. Around that time, he met Moira Shearer, a famous ballerina, who later became his wife, and together they had four children.

Sir Ludovic decided that he wanted to become a Member of Parliament, so in 1956, he stood as the Liberal candidate for the town of Rochdale in the north of England. In the election, he did very well, but not well enough to win, so he gave up his ambition to become a politician and returned to journalism. He went on to campaign for euthanasia and also to support people who were sent to prison for crimes they didn't commit.

11.3

a Look at the first part of the tapescript (until ... *where I studied economics.*) Listen and practise reading the text at the same time. Don't worry about the hesitations (for example *erm* ...). Practise reading it until you feel confident.

b Underline phrases in the tapescript which mean

1 the next thing I did was to go to university
2 to become a member of
3 I really didn't like it at all
4 I enjoyed myself very much
5 I became famous
6 we produced the food we ate

11.4

a We often put certain adjectives before certain nouns. Look at these phrases from the tapescript.

(a) complete surprise
(a) real shock
(the) right decision
(a) big success

b Listen to the cassette. Notice how Elly stresses both words. Practise saying the phrases, paying attention to the stress.

c How do you say these phrases in your language?

11.5

a Listen to the sentences. Notice the intonation on the stressed words.

I was hoping to work in television, but in the end, I got a job in radio.

I was planning to travel a lot, but I ended up getting married and settling down.

b Say the sentences, paying attention to the stress and intonation.

11.6

There are several time expressions in the tapescript (e.g. *towards the end of his time there*). Underline as many as you can. Check with the answer key.

How would you say these expressions in your language?

11.6

Look at these words from tapescript 11.7. We can put them into three groups, according to how we pronounce -*ed*.

1 distinguished, finished
   -*ed* is pronounced /t/
2 managed, joined
   -*ed* is pronounced /d/
3 decided, interrupted
   -*ed* is pronounced /ɪd/

Look at these other words finishing in -*ed*. Which group do they belong to?

3 educated	☐ washed
☐ studied	☐ hated
☐ worked	☐ stopped
☐ lived	☐ ended
☐ watched	☐ laughed
☐ married	☐ phoned
☐ returned	☐ started
☐ translated	☐ carried

twelve

12.1

There's a very successful lawyer and he, he bought a brand new, very expensive car and er, he parked it in front of the office, and he was ready to show it off to all his colleagues.

And he was getting out, and a new car came along very close to him and tore the door off the car. So the lawyer was furious, er, he rang the police, and the policeman arrived about two minutes later, and the man was still furious. He, he said, 'Look at my car, I only got it this morning, and it cost me a fortune. What a disaster!'

The policeman looked at him and he said, 'I don't believe this! You people – you are so materialistic. You only think about your cars and your money and your smart hotels. Look, don't you realize, it's not just your car, look, look there, look – you've lost your arm.'

And the lawyer looked down at his empty sleeve and he said, 'Oh no! Oh, this is terrible. Where's my gold watch?'

12.2

S I went to that new Italian restaurant, you know, the one, the one on the corner ...

L Hm, yes, I know.

S ... and I had a really good meal there, 'cos it's excellent food. Er, I paid for it and I, and I came home (Mm) and then as I came through the door, when I got home, I realized that I'd lost the wallet.

L Oh, no!

S And I'd no idea where it was, could have been in the restaurant, I might have dropped it on the way home, (Oh) I thought somebody might have even picked my pocket (Yeah) and of course, it had, er, it had my name and address in it, (Oh, yes) my telephone number, and about £50 in cash.

Two days later, I got a phone call, and this man said, 'Oh, is that Sam Davis?' (Mm) So I said, 'Yes.' (Mm) 'Have you lost a wallet?' (Oh!) he said, so I thought, 'Yes, I have, yes, (Mm) yes, have you found it?' And he said, 'I have.' Er, I said, 'Well, can you get it back to me?' (Hmm) He said, 'OK, I'll send it to you.'

And sure enough, a few days later in the post ... wallet arrived!

L Gosh!

S So I opened it, (Yeah) the money had been taken out, (Oh) yeah, and he'd put a note inside it. It said, 'Be more careful.'

L Oh, what a cheek! Ooh.

S Well, you live and learn.

L Yeah.

12.3

I suddenly remembered I'd left the gas on.
She realized that she'd met him before.
I found out later that he'd been in prison.
When the film started, I realized that I'd already seen it.

12.4

S Well, I went for a walk one morning, (Yeah) and suddenly realized I'd left my keys at home. The only other keys were with my husband, (Hmm) and he was at work. So anyway, I phoned my daughter on the mobile (Yeah) and erm, I said, 'Look, I'm locked out, I don't know what to do.' And then all of a sudden, the battery went dead. (Oh, no) I know. So anyway, then I decided to walk to my husband's workplace.

C To get the key, yeah, yeah.

S Yeah, exactly. Anyway, but listen to this, meanwhile my daughter had arranged for a taxi to collect the keys from my husband (Hmm) and take them to the house. (Oh, no) I know! So when the taxi arrives, nobody was there, so the driver posted the keys through the letter box! (Oh!) What a nightmare!

C Oh, dear!

12.5

SA Hello, do you need any help?

C Oh, erm, thanks but no, no, I'm just looking.

SA OK, fine, erm, just give me a shout if you want any help.

C Oh, sorry, excuse me, have you got this in any other colours? I'm really looking for something a little bit darker than this.

SA Oh, yeah, OK, um, might as well have a look under here. I've got it in dark green.

C Mm, ah, yes.

SA Is it, is it medium you want?

C Yes, that's lovely. Er, (yep) where can I try it on?

SA Oh, er ... the changing room's just over there.

C Oh, oh fine, yes I see it, thanks.

SA How are you getting on?

C Mm, well, actually, I'm afraid it doesn't fit very well.

SA Oh, no!

C No, it's a bit tight under the arms.

SA Hm. Well, er, we've got it in other sizes. Do you want to try on another one?

C No, er, well, actually in fact, I don't think it suits me really.

SA Right.

C I'll just have another look around.

SA Sure.

12.2

Cover the tapescript.
Sam made three guesses about
what had happened to his wallet.
Complete the gaps.

1 It _____ (be) in the
   restaurant.
2 I _____ (drop) it on
   the way home.
3 I thought somebody
   _____ (pick) my
   pocket.

Check with the tapescript.

12.3

a Listen to the sentences. Underline
   the words which are stressed.

b Practise saying the sentences,
   paying attention to the stress.

12.4

a Listen to the cassette. How many
   times does she say the word
   anyway? How do you say *anyway* in
   your language?

b There are other common words
   and expressions that we use when
   we tell a story. Look at the
   tapescript, and underline the
   following

   1 well
   2 so
   3 then
   4 all of a sudden
   5 but listen to this
   6 meanwhile

   How do you say these expressions
   in your language?

12.5

Look at the first line of the
conversation between the customer
and the shop assistant, but cover
the rest of the tapescript. Try to
predict the next line.

Now look at the first two lines, but
cover the rest of the tapescript. Can
you predict the third line?
Continue like this until the end of
the tapescript.

twelve money matters

SA Oh, have you found something?

C Yes, I'll take this one. Oh, oh, these are nice! Ooh, they're lovely. Actually, I could get these as a present for someone. How much are they?

SA Er, 15.95.

C 15.95 – yes, I'll have these as well. Erm, I'll take two. Could you wrap them up for me please?

SA Yes, of course.

C OK, now, er, can I use my credit card?

SA Absolutely.

12.6
Part 1

When I was getting married, (Mm) erm, I had this stunning pink dress, (Mm) and I really needed a beautiful hat to go with it, and I looked everywhere and couldn't find anything, and then one day, I was in town, and I saw the perfect hat in this shop, went in and saw the price tag and thought, 'No, I can't possibly afford it.'

So I was in town again working the next week and noticed there was a sale on, (Ah) went in, looked at the price of the hat. It was much cheaper (Mm) but still pretty expensive. The wedding was coming up, I still hadn't found a hat to go with the dress. I was getting worried. I went past that shop again a week later, and she had actually reduced the hat. (Ah!) So I went in and I said, 'Thank goodness, I can afford to buy this hat now,' bought it, wore it at the wedding. It looked stunning, I thought. I knew my husband hated it. (Oh!) But everybody commented on it, (Yes) and er, it was a huge success.

Part 2

Er, but funnily enough, er, after about three months of marriage, we were going to a big party. (Mm) I thought, 'Where's that wonderful hat? I'll wear it.' Couldn't find it anywhere. Went outside to do a bit of gardening, and we've got a horse down in the field at the bottom of our house. I noticed the horse was wearing my pink hat. (Oh, I don't believe it!) My husband had cut two holes in the top of it, stuck the horse's ears through it (Oh no!) and that was the end of that! The horse looked great!

12.6

When we tell stories, we often use time phrases. Match time phrases from the text to the stages in the story.

1 The beginning of the story.
   When I was getting married …

2 Elspeth sees the hat for the first time.
   _____

3 Elspeth sees there is a sale.
   _____

4 The price of the hat is reduced again, and so Elspeth buys it.
   _____

5 Elspeth wears the hat.
   _____

6 Elspeth looks for the hat again to wear it to a party.
   _____

12.6

The words below contain the sounds you've studied in this listening booklet. Practise saying the words, paying attention to the pronunciation of the sound indicated.

came /eɪ/	_____
cars /ɑː/	_____
man /æ/	_____
materialistic /ə/	_____
best /e/	_____
police /iː/	_____
him /ɪ/	_____
eye /aɪ/	_____
door /ɔː/	_____
close /əʊ/	_____
cost /ɒ/	_____
money /ʌ/	_____
put /ʊ/	_____
true /uː/	_____
girl /ɜː/	_____
there /eə/	_____
brother /ð/	_____
think /θ/	_____
eats /s/	_____
brings /z/	_____
show /ʃ/	_____
church /tʃ/	_____
just /dʒ/	_____
arrived /d/	_____
parked /t/	_____
wanted /ɪd/	_____

Next to each word, write another word with the same sound, for example

came /eɪ/   play _____

Check your answers in a dictionary.

1.3

Ralph shows he is listening: Oh, right!
Lily shows she is listening: Yeah; Oh, yeah; Is she?; Oh, maybe not ...
Lily shows surprise/horror: Oh no!

1 queueing up ... the other day
2 beside
3 have a look at
4 for a while
5 being really horrible / nasty to

1.4

pub, night, really extraordinary conversation, man, young guy, shaved head, came, told, bank robber

1.4

/æ/	mad, exactly, bank, stand
/eɪ/	take, came, stranger, conversation
/ɑː/	father, park, market, path
/ə/	asleep, burglar, ago, important

1.7

studying: at school; I'm studying physics, chemistry and biology; leave school; go to university; to study medicine; doing part of the course; better teaching there; better courses or universities; training; a year out; studied

going abroad: in the States; going overseas; abroad; over there; in Australia; a different country; another city

1.9

questions: Where are you from? Oh, really? Whereabouts? Are you travelling by yourself? Are you meeting somebody, perhaps? And you, you're meeting somebody, maybe? Really? What do you do?
positive adjectives: lovely, nice, interesting, beautiful, fascinating, adventurous

2.2

tiny	/ˈtaɪni/
circular	/ˈsɜːkjələ/
peaceful	/ˈpiːsfl/
quiet	/ˈkwaɪət/
frightened	/ˈfraɪtnd/
frightening	/ˈfraɪtnɪŋ/

coracles they're circular, almost like a dish
a microlite it's like a hang glider

2.3

summer, last, holiday, Cuba, spent, time, capital city, Havana, cheapest, best, city, cycle rickshaws, have, cabin, attached, bicycle, seat, people

2.3

/iː/	seat, cheap, people, these
/e/	red, them, definite, get
/ə/	cinema, after, international, mother
/eɪ/	grey, steak, break, weigh

2.4

im**por**tant   a**cc**o**mm**odation   pri**o**rity
ad**ven**ture   ex**ci**tement

2.6

stage 1: Come in ... What can I do for you?
stage 2: Um, my washing machine isn't working properly.
stage 3: Oh dear ... the powder isn't being used.
stage 4: Right, well, listen ... About 9.30.
stage 5: OK, lovely ... Thank you.

3.4

... they were tremendous fun to work with ...
That sounds fun!
It was great fun ...

1	kinds	4	few	7	awful
2	quite	5	loads	8	sorts
3	bit	6	lot		

3.5

I've done lots of different things; I've done radio; I've done television jobs; I've been in quite a few television programmes; I've done theatre; I've even done some work in advertising; I've met some interesting people; I've had a really good time; Who've I met?; I've had a good time.

3.5

/ɪ/	Italy, interesting, did, thing, different
/aɪ/	quite, while, hide, high, night, advertise
/iː/	police, pizza, sardine, skiing

3.7

1 When I was at primary school
2 When I was a child
3 When I left school
4 when I was younger
5 When I was in my early twenties

4.5

1	in	2	in	3	to
4	on	5	to		

par**ti**cular   **pro**gramme   inte**res**ted
pre**sen**ter   sur**vi**val
rainforest   **ca**mera   **na**tural
hyp**no**sis   psy**cho**logist

4.6

You're happy with that, are you?
But what about your idea for ... ?
... what do you think?

4.6

/əʊ/	programme, home, go, local, also
/ɒ/	possibility, costs, not, lock, politics, won
/ɔː/	store, door, court, for, bought
/ʌ/	love, young, mother, some

4.8

Anne uses these expressions to show she agrees with Chris.

5.4

was /wəz/; at /ət/; as /əz/

we had these neighbours (first mention)

You've been asked to this drinks party (first mention)

we all went to this, to this party (mentioned before)

there was this knock at the door (first mention)

5.5

a terrible, elegant, beautiful, expensive, floor length, long, silk, huge, lovely, relaxed, casual

b terrible – the situation; elegant – the wedding; beautiful, expensive, floor length, long, elegant, silk – her dress; huge, elegant – her hat; lovely – the place; relaxed, casual – the wedding

5.5

/ʌ/	butter, much, judge, cupboard, sun
/ʊ/	put, should, push, pudding, bull
/uː/	rude, use, true, juice

5.7

maga<u>zi</u>nes, <u>ca</u>refully, mis<u>ta</u>ke, ciga<u>re</u>ttes, <u>chil</u>dren, <u>some</u>times, im<u>por</u>tant, re<u>mem</u>ber, abso<u>lute</u>ly, i<u>den</u>tity

6.3

a ... the main advantage of working in a family business ...

... another advantage is working ...

There are disadvantages as well.

... what are the disadvantages, then?

I suppose the disadvantage of my situation ...

b advantage /əd'vɑːntɪdʒ/, disadvantage /dɪsəd'vɑːntɪdʒ/

c of

d the main ... ; another ... ; there are ... ; what are the ... ?

6.5

uh yes; er; oh, oh yes; oh right, great, OK; erm; well; yeah OK

6.5

1 twenty-third	5 earn	9 certainly

2 turkey	6 girl's	10 word
3 hers	7 Thursday	
4 world	8 learn	

7.2

a **Jonathan** There's something I've been meaning to say; it's only a small thing; it's just that

Ann I do want to talk to you about something, though, that's erm, (mm) that's been on my mind er, recently. Erm it's quite difficult for me to say, really; The thing is, ...

Both speakers aren't very direct at all.

b I'm really trying to concentrate
definition 2

It's quite difficult for me to say, really
definition 1

I don't really think that we have a lot in common
definition 4

(Hmm) really
definition 1

we haven't really got that much in common
definition 4

7.6

a is, meet, has, comes, helps, realize, are, feels, thinks, realizes, doesn't want, goes, think

b /s/ helps, thinks
/z/ is, has, comes, feels, doesn't, goes
/ɪz/ realizes

7.6

pair / pear; stair / stare; fair / fare; there / their; air / heir; where / wear; bare / bear

8.2

a Could is pronounced /kʊd/

b do, favour, give, hand, do

8.3

a are /ə/

b My goodness! Wow, that sounds exciting. Next Friday! Hey, that's great.
... gosh, Kazakhstan!

8.8

1	dropped	6	check
2	cut	7	send
3	worry	8	right
4	wanted	9	vegetarian
5	on	10	help yourself

8.8

/ð/ together, this, those, mother, then, there, these

/θ/ three, thirty, thin, both, healthy, thick, thirsty, teeth, with

9.2

If I had more time, like on holiday, for example, I'd have a very long, slow, lazy lunch.

If I had a cleaner, things'd be different and the place might just get tidy quicker.

9.3

1	ages	4	need	7	day
2	toast	5	day	8	wake
3	cup of tea	6	miss		

9.5

/s/ hats, books, chips, forks, lips, biscuits, tights

/z/ chairs, pens, magazines, mountains, toys, clouds, windows

10.4

a them /ðəm/

10.5

shirt (1), bridge (3), cheap (2), chef (1), cheque (2), jump (3), chocolate (2), joke (3), ashtray (1), jazz (3), architecture (2), station (1), garage (3), British (1), chicken (2)

10.6

Do you <u>fancy</u> going <u>out</u> for a <u>meal</u> tonight?
<u>How</u> about coming <u>over</u> for a <u>drink</u> this <u>evening</u>?
I was <u>wondering</u> if you'd <u>like</u> to see a <u>film</u>.

10.7

a 1 **they greet each other** I'm so sorry! ... Oh, fine.

   2 **they give and accept reasons for being late** I got horribly stuck ... Forget it! All right.

   3 **they order a drink** Can I get you a drink? ... Just an orange juice.

b horribly / absolutely terrible / terrible
   miles away / five streets away
   Forget it / just forget it / Forget it!

11.3

1 I went on to university
2 to join
3 I hated every minute of it
4 I had the best time of my life
5 I became a household name
6 we grew our own food

11.6

1 towards the end of his time there
2 in 1938
3 in a day
4 at the time
5 then
6 when war broke out the following year
7 After the war
8 then
9 first
10 later
11 Around that time
12 later
13 in 1956

11.6

educated (3), washed (1), studied (2), hated (3), worked (1), stopped (1), lived (2), ended (3), watched (1), laughed (1), married (2), phoned (2), returned (2), started (3), translated (3), carried (2)

12.3

suddenly, remembered, left, gas
realized, met, before
found, later, been, prison
film, started, realized, already, seen

12.6

1 When I was getting married
2 then, one day
3 the next week
4 a week later
5 at the wedding
6 after about three months of marriage

OXFORD
UNIVERSITY PRESS

Great Clarendon Street, Oxford OX2 6DP

Oxford University Press is a department of the
University of Oxford.

It furthers the University's objective of
excellence in research, scholarship, and
education by publishing worldwide in

Oxford New York

Auckland Bangkok Buenos Aires Cape Town
Chennai Dar es Salaam Delhi Hong Kong
Istanbul Karachi Kolkata Kuala Lumpur
Madrid Melbourne Mexico City Mumbai
Nairobi São Paulo Shanghai Singapore Taipei
Tokyo Toronto

with an associated company in Berlin

Printed in China

Acknowledgements

The Publisher and Authors would like to
thank the following for permission to
reproduce photographs:

Getty images: cover (Whit Preston / blue sky),
cover and title page (Uwe Krejci / 2 people)